BUFFET STYLE

Home Entertaining & Party Ideas

more quick and easy recipes

for casual entertaining

by Robert Zollweg

Written and Designed by Robert Zollweg
Photography by Rick Luettke, Luettke Studio.com
Graphics by Gary Raschke and Robert Zollweg

Art Direction Gary Raschke

Library of Congress Cataloging-in-Publication Data:

Buffet Style - Home Entertaining & Party Ideas
by Robert Zollweg

ISBN 978-0-692-23500-3

Printed in the United States
by R.R. Donnelley and Company

This book is dedicated to

Fran Breitner
Once in a lifetime there is a coworker and a great friend
and
Art, Nancy, Dana, Angela and Nicolle for seeing my vision

To all my family:
Steve, Virginia, Rhonda & Doug, Christopher & Sandy,
Elaine & Tom, Judy & Carl, Richard & Sandy,
Kaylie, Korrin, Andrew, Bret and Morgan

Gary Raschke, what an art director; Rick Luettke, the best photographer

Steve Tester, Vicki Richardson, Fran Breitner and Bill Muzzillo for their editing skills

To all my Libbey associates
Gina Baccari. Beth Baroncini, Cathie Logan, Kelly Kelley,
Sally Bendetti, Amy Pownall, Tina Schneider, Leigh McCarter,
Karen Barentzen, Roger Williams, Serena Williams,
Jeff Joyce, Derek Fielding, Greg Pax

Sandy Shultz, Melissa Fleig, Emily West, Fred Amstel

Angela Cross-Braswell, Dawn Aurand, Kimberly Rutkowski, Diane Shinaberry,
Amy Miles, Brooks Clayton, Jennifer LaPlante, Lisa Fell, Tony Gardner,
Joe Mefferd and Allen Hutton

And to all my Libbey associates. You're the best !

Home Entertaining

Contents

Introduction   8 - 9

Serving Presentations   10 - 15

Entertaining Tips   16 - 21

Dinnerware, Serveware and Bakeware   22 - 27

Theme Buffets Ideas   28 - 29
Birthday   30 - 37
Mexican Fiesta   38 - 45
Tapas & Tastings   46 - 53
Chocolate Dessert Party   54 - 59
Holiday Buffet Dinner   60 - 67
Thanksgiving-Fall Harvest   68 - 77
Fourth of July Celebration   78 - 83
St. Patrick's Day   84 - 89
Halloween Ghosts & Goblins   90 - 95
New Year's Eve Celebration   96 - 103
Healthy Options Cocktail Party   104 - 111
Baby or Bridal Shower   112 - 117
Super Sports Party   118 - 123

Index   124 - 125

Introduction

Buffet Style - Home Entertaining is a simple cookbook, with a lot of tips and ideas on serving theme buffets and using wonderful quick and easy recipes for preparing an incredible Tasting Party or Family Buffet in your home. You can use all the wonderful products we have put together to serve these entrees, desserts, appetizers and cocktails with incredible flair.

Having all the right serving pieces makes these tasting parties or buffets all the more enjoyable. Your guests will feel right at home and enjoy every minute of your time together.

But it goes beyond just the entrees, desserts, appetizers and cocktails. It's about serving all of these in a variety of containers and most of all, it's about presentation. You probably wouldn't bother having a tasting party or setting up a buffet table for just 2 or 3 people, but you would when it's about having a great cocktail party or any get together for all your friends and family. Making your guests feel welcome and at home is what entertaining is all about and recipes from **Buffet Style - Home Entertaining** is here to help.

Most of the following recipes are pretty quick and simple to make. This is important with today's lifestyle in home entertaining. Nobody has the time or patience to spend hours in the kitchen preparing and cleaning up from a complicated recipe. This is a little unfortunate, but true. But remember, setting up for a tasting party or family buffet is supposed to be fun and enjoyable. So keep it simple and prepare what you are comfortable making.

Displaying these tastings or buffet layouts is a key component in entertaining. Presenting them on a variety of different serving and tiered trays helps with this fashionable and trendy presentation. See a few photos on the following pages for a few creative ideas. These presentations are great for special parties, weddings, showers and birthdays, to name a few. You will look very professional and your guests will look forward to another one of your parties or get togethers.

I hope you enjoy all of these unique presentations, along with some wonderful dessert, appetizer and cocktail recipes, as much as I have in creating them.

I love to entertain and theme parties and buffets are a great way to turn an occasion into something really special using all the wonderful dinnerware and serveware accessories shown on the following pages.

Enjoy !

Robert Zollweg

Serving Presentations
Coffee and Dessert Buffet

Serving Buffet Style

Serving food in a buffet style setting is perfect for large get togethers or even some smaller ones, but both will work well when you have limited seating and want all your guests to have a variety or selection of different foods and drinks.

Try using a couple of glass tiered serving pieces and casseroles, some ceramic rectangular serving trays and, of course, a variety of different foods. Compliment your buffet with special coffees, teas, dessert wines, cognacs or flavored liqueurs served in small cordial glasses. Remember, it's all about presentation and making your guests feel special and at home.

For a fabulous dessert or buffet table, you can use your kitchen counter, dining room table or even a small card table set up in the living room or family room, wherever you decide to serve. The little extra effort with your presentation makes all the difference in the world.

On the following few pages, you'll find some creative ideas for setting up various buffets with dinnerware and serveware pieces in various locations throughout your home.

Cocktail Party

A little cocktail party doesn't need to be a big deal. Clean off your kitchen counter, add a small lamp for ambiance, add some of your favorite wines or cocktails and several little appetizers or desserts. It's that simple and see how special it looks.

Your dining room table is a perfect place to serve food for a large gathering of friends and family. Whether you cook it all yourself or make it a potluck, special foods, served and arranged properly make all the difference in the world.

Coffee and Dessert Buffet

A simple card table covered with a special tablecloth is all you need to set up a coffee and dessert buffet anywhere in your home. It is perfect after coming home from the theater or when your family or friends have just finished playing cards. It's a perfect little setting your guests will be sure to notice.

Wine and Cheese Buffet

Such little effort is all it takes to set up a small wine and cheese buffet somewhere in your home. It can be a simple platter of cheese and grapes, some small sandwiches or chicken kabobs. Make them yourself or just buy them from your local grocery store delicatessen. Either way, entertaining buffet style is simple and easy and looks fabulous !

Entertaining Tips

This item has a multitude of uses, from a cake plate, punch bowl, vegetable server, covered relish tray to a salad bowl with space for extra veggies. What a great addition to your collection of everyday serveware.

Vertical Serving

When space is limited, use a couple of 3 tiered servers for all those fancy cookies, cupcakes or appetizers along with a footed trifle bowl or platter. It looks fabulous and you will have extra room for all the other foods and cocktails.

Buffet Ideas

I like to use these sign holders to identify all my different foods so guests will know what is what (especially when you have a vegetarian or peanut-free dish).

Another space saving idea for a buffet is to use 3-4 small square vases to hold your flatware. I like using clear glass because the handles are up and my guests can see what utensils are in each container. Try folding your napkins in another vase or rolled up with your flatware inside the napkins (like you see in so many restaurants) and place them inside a vase. For those crafty types, add a festive ribbon around each vase to co-ordinate with your party theme.

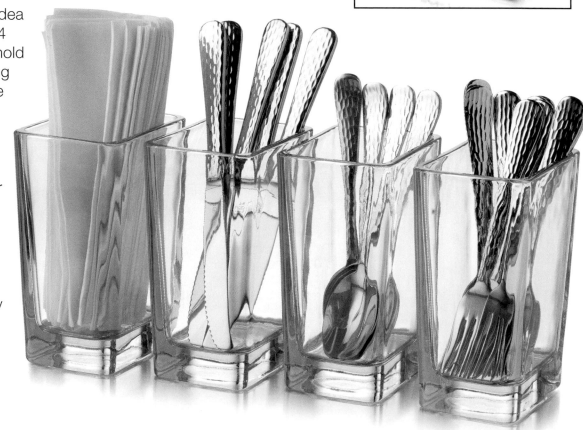

Coffee Service

When serving coffee and tea for your guests, the ideal setup is to have a thermos of coffee and one for hot water and a variety of coffee and tea cups, along with plenty of sugar, sweeteners and cream, maybe even some artificial

Buffet Table Layouts

Here's a golden rule for any type of buffet dinner: always have the dinner plates at the beginning and the napkins and flatware at the end. This way, your guests can pick up a plate, select the food they want and then pick up their napkin and flatware and be seated. If you group them together, they will pick everything up at one time and then have to juggle all of it while trying to serve themselves. So remember: plates at one end, napkins and flatware at the other. Your guests will notice what a great host or hostess you are.

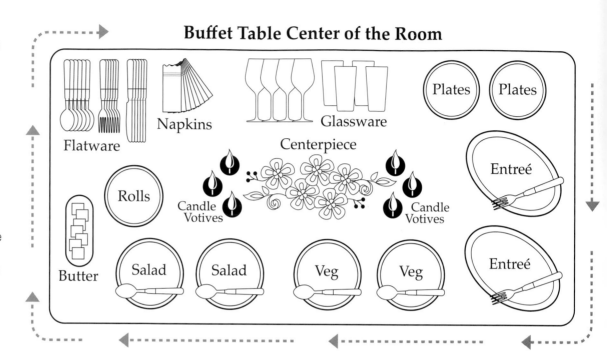

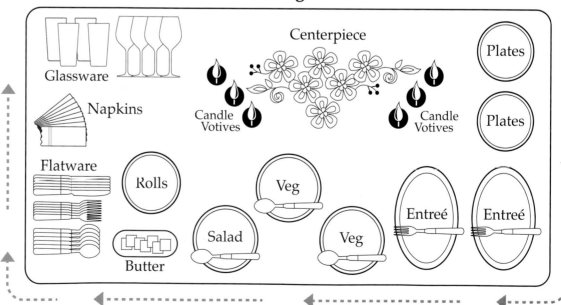

More Tips For Perfect Entertaining

- Always plan for a little more food than you have invited guests. Running out of food, especially the main entree, is a real no no.

- Plan a conversation starter, something fun and entertaining.

- Have plenty of different beverages available and know your guests' likes and dislikes.

- I like buffets and tasting parties because you can make a little something that will suit everyone, especially for a large gathering of mixed people. So have a variety of different entrees and side dishes.

- Don't plan beyond your culinary skills or the time you have. You'll drive yourself nuts and your guests will feel uncomfortable.

- Have an easy accessible location for coats, or even hire a coat check person for larger get togethers and a convenient place to put them.

- Have some soft, contemporary music in the background, just loud enough to notice but not so loud as to distract from the conversation.

- Make sure you have plenty of parking with security. I have even hired a teenager with an umbrella or two, in case of rain. The ladies will love you for it.

- Always make your guests feel comfortable and engaged in conversation. Find the shy ones and make it a point to include them at some point in the conversation.

Dinnerware, Serveware and Bakeware

Glass Dinnerware

A stack of glass dinnerware is perfect for your next buffet. It's inexpensive, looks great and fits easily into your dishwasher. What more could you ask for? Ceramic pieces are quite beautiful as well. Almost everyone prefers glass or ceramic over paper or plastic, and besides, it's more green !

Glass Dinnerware, Serveware and Flatware

The combination of your glass dinnerware along with your glass and ceramic serving pieces will provide a great food presentation for your guests and they will be very impressed with the look of your buffet.

Glass Serveware with Acaciawood

Glass Bakeware
with Bamboo Trivets

Theme Buffet Ideas

Birthday Celebration
30-37

Holiday Buffet Dinner
60-67

Halloween Ghosts & Goblins
90-95

New Years Eve Celebration
96-103

Mexican Fiesta
38-45

Tapas & Tasting Party
46-53

Chocolate Dessert Party
54-59

Thanksgiving Fall Harvest
68-77

Fourth of July Celebration
78-83

St. Patrick's Day
84-89

Healthy Options Cocktail Party
104-111

Baby or Bridal Shower
112-117

Super Sports Party
118-123

Birthday
Celebration
recipes and party ideas

Ice Cream Cake

This is definitely one of our family favorites. I borrowed this recipe from Elaine Bender. She has been making this for years and it is very popular at all our family get togethers and birthday celebrations.

You can use any flavor of cake or ice cream. Try white cake with strawberry ice cream or chocolate cake with either chocolate chip, black cherry or chocolate mint ice cream. Each one makes a uniquely different ice cream dessert.

Recipe

1 box cake mix (any flavor)
3/4 gallon ice cream, slightly softened
32 oz whipped topping (it comes in regular, chocolate and strawberry flavor)

Bake the cake mix in 2 round or square cake pans according to the package. Let cool.

Place the first layer of the cake on a footed serving platter. Evenly spread the ice cream to cover the layer of cake. Add the second layer of cake. Fluff the whipped topping with a spoon. Cover the entire 2 layer cake with whipped topping. Put in the freezer until set. Cover it with plastic wrap. You can make this a few days ahead if you are having a birthday party.

When ready to serve, remove from freezer about 30 minutes before serving. It will make cutting into slices a lot easier.

Pictured on the right is a strawberry confetti cake with creamy strawberry ice cream in the center, covered with whipped topping and garnished with fresh strawberries.

Serve and Enjoy !

This is such a festive way to serve an ice cream sundae for a larger group of people or ideal for a birthday party. It makes a great presentation and tastes just wonderful. You can make it with any flavor of ice cream, although when using vanilla ice cream, you can see all the layering and center fillings.

You will need one glass or metal ring pan, some plastic wrap and all the ingredients listed below.

Party Ring Surprise

Recipe

1 gallon ice cream (any flavor) softened
some ice cream toppings (chocolate syrup, hot fudge, caramel, strawberry, etc.)
4 oz toffee pieces, mini chocolate chips, chopped peanuts or pecans
some plastic wrap

Using a glass or metal ring pan, line the ring pan with plastic wrap. Place in freezer for 10 minutes so the plastic wrap really clings to the pan. Fill the ring pan about half full with the softened ice cream, smooth down. Add any condiments you like. I like to add hot fudge, caramel and chopped pecans. Cover or fill the remaining ring pan with ice cream. You can even use two different kinds of ice cream, like chocolate on the bottom and vanilla on the top as pictured above.

Place ring pan in freezer for a few hours. When ready to serve, remove from freezer, let stand a few minutes and gently lift the ice cream dessert out of the pan using the plastic wrap. Place upside down on the flat surface of a cake plate or platter. Carefully remove the plastic wrap. Drizzle with a little topping and sprinkle with nuts or toffee pieces. Serve immediately. Store any leftovers in the freezer.

Enjoy !

Ice Cream Sundaes

Why even mention simple everyday ice cream sundaes? Because they are perfect for any birthday party, young or not so young. They are refreshing and can be made with any flavor of ice cream. They will also compliment just about any kind of cake.

Try serving them with several small bowls with a variety of toppings, like chopped peanuts, chocolate chips, granola, M&M's, gummy bears or any small candy pieces.

This recipe will make several ice cream sundaes.

Recipe

Here is what you will need:

> 1/2 gallon of your favorite flavor of ice cream
> some toppings: chocolate syrup, hot fudge, strawberry, caramel, etc.
> some whipped topping
> several maraschino cherries, optional
> some sugar or vanilla wafers, optional

In any size ice cream sundae dish, start with a small scoop of your special flavor of ice cream, then add some of your favorite toppings. More than one is ok. Add another scoop of ice cream and more toppings. Complete it with a large dollop of whipped topping and a maraschino cherry.

Serve and Enjoy !

Party Punch will add a lot of pizzazz to any party and is great for when you need to serve a lot of kids and adults all at one time.

This recipe will make enough to fill a large punch bowl. You may need to adjust the quantities of the ingredients to fit the size of your container. Use white wine or vodka. I love to use red during the holidays, because it's so traditional and adds a real feeling of family and being together.

Omit the alcohol for a non-alcoholic punch.

Party Punch

Recipe
Here is what you will need:

4 liters of club soda, ginger ale or lemon lime soda
2 bottles of dark red wine, like a Merlot or Cabernet
3-4 cups cranberry or cranapple juice
One orange, one lemon, one lime, sliced
Handful of fresh cranberries, raspberries and blueberries
4 cups ice cubes

Several oranges, lemons or limes for garnish, jar of maraschino cherries and some toothpicks, optional

Put all the fresh fruit in the bottom of your punch bowl. Add the soda and whatever alcoholic beverage you want. Add the ice and stir carefully. I take a slice of fruit and a cherry on a toothpick and put one inside each of my punch glasses and arrange on a festive tray or all around the punch bowl. Serve along with your favorite birthday cake or cupcakes.

Enjoy !

Banana Splits

Back when I was a kid, if you ordered a banana split at a soda fountain shop, this is what you got - a wonderful combination of chocolate, strawberry and vanilla ice cream with 3 different toppings and lots of whipped cream and a maraschino cherry on top. Back then it was the most over the top ice cream dessert on the menu. Probably still is, but worth every penny !

Here is another perfect ice cream dessert and a great compliment to your birthday party.

Recipe

Here is what you will need:

- 1 quart chocolate ice cream
- 1 quart vanilla ice cream
- 1/2 cup chocolate syrup
- 1/2 cup pineapple topping
- small jar of maraschino cherries
- 1 quart strawberry ice cream
- 6 bananas, sliced the long way
- 1/2 cup strawberry topping
- whipping cream or whipped topping

You can use almost any flavor of ice cream, but tradition suggests chocolate, vanilla and strawberry.

Start with a scoop of chocolate ice cream, then a scoop of vanilla and then a scoop of strawberry. Place a banana slice on each side of the dish. Put a spoonful of chocolate syrup over the chocolate ice cream, a spoonful of pineapple topping over the vanilla ice cream and finally, a spoonful of strawberry topping over the strawberry ice cream. Put a dollop of whipped topping on each scoop of ice cream and a maraschino cherry. Don't wait too long before you enjoy this delicious dessert. Serve and Enjoy !

This is a very smooth and refreshing dessert that is great for any party as well as for breakfast or brunch. Smoothies also make great after school snacks for the kids and can be made with almost any fruit.

This recipe will make 2-3 smoothies in any tall soda or hurricane glass.

party smoothies

Recipe

Here is what you will need:

2 cups vanilla ice cream or vanilla yogurt
1/2 cup whole milk
1 cup whipped topping
12 oz bag frozen mixed berries, thawed
1 cup crushed ice (optional)

To make a specific fruit flavor, just use 12 ounces or so of your favorite fresh or frozen fruit. The more you use, the stronger fruit flavor you will get.

Slightly chop or puree the mixed berries in the blender. Add the yogurt, milk and crushed ice. Blend well. Add the whipped topping, puree until smooth and creamy. Pour into tall smoothie glasses.

These are light and fluffy. Kids will love them, adults too.

Serve and Enjoy !

MEXICAN FIESTA

ENCHILADA CASSEROLE

This traditional Mexican-American casserole can be made either hot or mild, depending on how spicy you like things. I always make mine mild and serve it with some hot sauce or salsa on the side, so that my guests can adjust it to their taste.

You will need one large oval casserole or any standard 9x13 baking dish.

Bake at 350 degrees

Recipe

12 corn or flour tortillas
2 cups shredded colby or cheddar cheese
1 small onion, finely chopped
1 cup chopped lettuce
non stick cooking spray

1 lb cooked ground beef, turkey or shredded chicken
1 jar or 2 cups enchilada sauce or regular salsa
1 green pepper, finely chopped
1 can refried beans, optional
sour cream and hot sauce on the side, optional

Lightly spray your casserole with cooking spray. Put a cup of enchilada sauce on the bottom. Place a tortilla shell flat on the table, spread about a tablespoon of refried beans, fill it with your choice of meat, lettuce, onion, green peppers and a heaping spoonful of enchilada sauce. Roll up and place in the casserole. Repeat this until you have filled the casserole. Cover with enchilada sauce and shredded cheddar/colby cheese.

Bake in oven at 350 degrees for 30-35 minutes until bubbly. This casserole is ideal when served with fresh salad and Mexican rice. Serve with sour cream and hot sauce on the side.

Enjoy !

Nothing is more perfect for a festive and refreshing Mexican Party than a punch bowl full of margarita punch. It is quick and simple and tastes fantastic.

You can make a traditional punch with lime juice, or jazz it up with strawberry or mandarin orange.

MARGARITA PUNCH

Recipe

You will need:

3 cans frozen limeade
6 cans of water
1 bottle of tequila
12 oz of Triple Sec
1/2 cup sugar
6-8 fresh limes & lemons, sliced
lots of crushed ice
one container of margarita rim salt, optional
several lime wedges for rimming

In a large punch bowl, carefully add the 3 cans of frozen limeade, water and sugar. Mix well. Add the tequila and triple sec and stir. Add the limes and lemons and several cups of crushed ice. Place the lime wedges in a small bowl next to the container of rimming salt. Your guests can rim the punch glass with lime juice and then dip the glass into the salt.

Fill with margarita punch and Enjoy !

HOMEMADE DEL SALSA

Nothing is more delicious than fresh homemade salsa. It just does not compare to the jar stuff and it is a whole lot better for you to boot!

There are a lot of versions of salsa. This one is mild but can be adjusted with adding a little hot sauce.

This will make about 3 cups of salsa.

Recipe

You will need the following ingredients:

6-7 fresh ripe tomatoes	one onion, finely chopped, about 1/2 cup
2 small garlic gloves, minced	1/2 cup chopped cilantro
4 tbsp fresh lime juice	salt & pepper to taste
1-2 Serrano or Jalapeno chili peppers, seeded and chopped	

In a large mixing bowl, mix together the finely chopped tomatoes (remove seeds and liquid first, be careful and avoid touching your eyes while chopping the chili's), chopped onion, garlic, cilantro. Add the lime juice, salt, pepper and chopped chilis. Be careful when chopping the chilis not to touch your eyes and then wash your hands immediately. Mix together and refrigerate for 2-3 hours. Serve with your favorite tostada chips or as a side with Mexican food.

Enjoy !

This layered taco salad is a perfect appetizer for almost any type of party. It takes a few minutes to put it all together, but in the end, it is well worth the effort. I modify it almost every time I make it by adding different ingredients. Sometimes I use sliced green olives, chopped cilantro or cooked whole kernel corn. Below is my basic recipe. It always turns out perfect.

TEQUILA TACO DIP

Recipe

Here is what you will need for ingredients:

one can refried beans
1 cup shredded iceberg lettuce
1 cup shredded cheddar cheese
1/2 cup, finely chopped black olives

1 cup sour cream
1 cup finely chopped tomatoes
2 cups salsa
large bag of tostada chips

In a mixing bowl add the refried beans, 3 tbsp of salsa and 2 tbsp of sour cream. Mix well. Spoon into a low profile serving bowl or platter and spread around to cover the platter. Spoon the remaining sour cream over the refried beans. It won't cover completely or look perfect. Sprinkle with the lettuce, then the tomatoes and drizzle with salsa in a basic layering effect. Sprinkle with the cheddar cheese and black olives. Serve immediately or cover with plastic wrap and refrigerate. Serve with your favorite tostada chips and a pitcher of margaritas.

Enjoy !

HOMEMADE GUACAMOLE

The name guacamole is derived from two Mexican Aztec words, ahuacati (avocado) and mole (sauce) and is made from fresh ripe avocados.

There is a Mexican restaurant in New York (Rosa Mexicana) that is famous for its homemade guacamole. I have watched them make it for years. Here is my version of their famous recipe. I hope to do it justice.

Recipe

Here is what you will need:

> 2 ripe avocados
> 1/2 cup red onion, chopped
> 2 tbsp cilantro, finely chopped
> 1 tbsp fresh lime juice
> 1 tomato, seeded and chopped
> 1/2 tsp coarse salt
> dash of pepper
> 1-2 Serrano chilies, seeded and minced

Slice the avocados in half and remove the large pit. Scoop out the meat of the avocado and place in a mixing bowl. Mash up coarsely. Carefully add the remaining ingredients and mix. Serve immediately or cover with plastic wrap and refrigerate. Covering it will keep it from turning brown until ready to serve. This will keep in the refrigerator for a few hours.

For a quick or speedy version: add 1/2 cup chunky salsa to the mashed avocado and serve.

Enjoy !

My sister, Judy, has been bringing this taco salad to our family get togethers for years. It is very tasty and will go with almost anything at any kind of party.

There are endless variations. I have even used chopped chicken breasts instead of the ground beef or no meat at all for a vegetarian version.

TACO SALAD

Recipe
Here is what you will need for ingredients:

one bag of tostada chips
one lb cooked ground beef, crumbled
2 cups chopped tomatoes
2 cups shredded cheddar cheese
1/2 cup chopped black olives
2 cups shredded iceberg lettuce
1/4 cup taco sauce or salsa

In a large serving bowl, break up the toasted chips into bite size pieces. Add the ground beef, tomatoes, black olives, shredded lettuce and cheddar cheese. Toss together. Sprinkle with taco sauce and carefully mix again.

Serve and Enjoy !

Tapas &
Tasting
Party

Kool Kabobs

Appetizer kabobs are pretty easy to make and you can use almost any type of cooked meat and vegetables to make a very delicious looking kabob.

Try using chicken, shrimp, beef, ham, sausage, mushrooms, green peppers, olives, pineapple, cheese, onions or cherry tomatoes.

Recipe
Ingredients:

2-3 chicken breasts, grilled
1 pkg Eckrich sausage, precooked
several mushrooms, sliced
20-24 long skewers

1 green pepper, chunked
fresh pineapple chunks
1/2 cup teriyaki sauce

You can also try a variety of different vegetables, grilled beef or shrimp

Take your skewer and place a piece of pineapple, chicken, mushroom, sausage, green pepper in any order. I'll mix up the order just to make them all look different. With a pastry brush (or even a new inexpensive paint brush) brush each kabob with teriyaki sauce. Place on a cookie sheet and place in the broiler oven for about 4-5 minutes until golden brown.

Place on a serving tray and Enjoy !

Here is a pretty basic recipe with some adjustments that will help to make it your own. There are so many different versions or variations of bruschetta around today.

I'll show you several different ingredients and give you some options on what to change or add to help you create something to call your own.

Bruschetta

Recipe

Start with the basic french baguette, thinly sliced and toasted. I've also used a thin sliced toasted rye bread with the crusts removed. Either one is perfect.

I spread each piece with some softened cream cheese with a little garlic salt added for some pizzazz. Then I layer either some finely sliced tomatoes or sliced cucumber, some finely chopped green onion and then sprinkle each with a little fresh parmesan cheese. To jazz it up a little more, add a slice of black or green olive, a little artichoke, fresh chopped cilantro or parsley and some fresh black pepper.

Serve and Enjoy !

Sassy Sangria

Sangria is to the Latin world what beer is to the Germans or wine to the French. I fell in love with sangria a few years ago after having it in a wonderful Tapas restaurant in the Flatiron District of New York, called Pipas on 19th Street. It can be made either red or white depending on the type of wine you use. This is an incredible party cocktail that your guests will just love. A pitcher of Sangria is a tradition that we take to the beach for sunsets. This will make enough for 4-6 servings in a 12 oz glass with ice.

Recipe

You will need a large glass punch bowl or pitcher and several glasses.

2 bottles of red wine
1 cup brandy or Cointreau
1 cup canned pears or peaches, mashed or pureed
1 orange, 1 lemon, 1 lime, all sliced
handful of blueberries, raspberries or strawberries
32 oz ginger ale or lemon lime soda
a couple cups of ice
a few fruit slices set aside for garnish

In the punch bowl, add the first five ingredients and mix well. Let this stand a few hours if you have time. When ready to serve, add the ginger ale and some ice and you are ready to go. Garnish with any type of fruit.

Serve and Enjoy !

*Non-alcoholic recipe: follow recipe from above but omit the red wine and brandy. In its place use one large container of cranberry or grape juice.

Serve and Enjoy !

Fatoush is a wonderful Mediterranean or Arabic salad that is used with various meats as a main entree. It also happens to be a great vegetarian main dish.

It is a great compliment to a variety of meats, especially lamb and chicken.

Famous Fatoush

Recipe
Ingredients:

2 English cucumbers, finely diced
1/2 red onion, finely chopped
baked pita chips
1 tbsp lemon juice
kosher salt and fresh ground pepper to taste

3 cup fresh cherry or grape tomatoes, halved
1/2 cup fresh Italian parsley, chopped
1/2 cup chopped fresh mint
1/2 cup crumbled feta cheese
dash of sumac

In a large mixing bowl, combine all the ingredients and toss gently. Break up the baked pita chips into small pieces. Add to the salad and mixed again. If you can not find baked pita chips, heat about one tablespoon of vegetable oil in a large skillet over medium heat. Place the pita pieces into the skillet and fry until golden brown. Blot dry with paper towel.

Adjust seasonings to taste. Serve and Enjoy !

Seafood Salad

This delicious salad is perfect for serving in small appetizer bowls for a tasting party. It is bursting with flavor and is a great compliment to your tasting party meat entrees.

Recipe

Ingredients:

- 1 cup small frozen salad shrimp, thawed
- 2 cups shredded cabbage
- 1 small can of crab meat
- 1 carrot, finely chopped
- 1/4 cup green onions, chopped
- 1 tbsp fresh parsley, chopped
- 1/4 cup poppyseed dressing

In a mixing bowl, add all the dry ingredients, shrimp and crab meat and toss. Add the poppyseed dressing a little at a time until it is well coated but not sloppy. Serve in individual tasting bowls.

Enjoy !

Spicy meatballs is another perfect tasting party appetizer especially when served on small tasting plates. What could look more special? It is just the right amount and a great compliment to seafood salad or fatoush.

Spicy Meatballs

Recipe

Here is what you will need:

1 lb frozen prepared meatballs
1/4 cup chopped green onions
1 cup orange marmalade preserves
1/4 cup honey
1/4 cup chopped sliced almonds
1 tbsp red pepper flakes
dash of soy sauce

Thaw the meatballs and heat in a microwaveable dish until hot. Set aside. In a mixing bowl, combine the green onions, chopped almonds, orange marmalade, honey and soy sauce. Mix thoroughly. Add the red pepper flakes to taste.

Pour this mixture over the hot meatballs and toss gently. Serve on small appetizer plates and drizzle any remaining sauce over each.

Serve and Enjoy !

CHOCOLATE DESSERT AND COFFEE BUFFET

CHOCOLATE MOUSSE

This is another rich and delicious, very easy chocolate dessert. You can make it with dark, semi-sweet or sweet chocolate, depending on the intensity of your desired chocolate flavor. I usually use semi-sweet chocolate. The mousse is sweet, but not too sweet. You will need 12 shot glasses (2 oz each) or small glass cordials.

Recipe

1 cup graham cracker crumbs, 3 tbsp butter and 1 tbsp sugar

one package (8 oz) cream cheese, softened
one container (8 oz) whipped topping
1/4 tsp vanilla
4 oz baking chocolate or chocolate chips
1 tbsp milk for melting chocolate

Melt butter in a microwavable bowl, add cracker crumbs and sugar, mix thoroughly. Place about a teaspoon of mixture in the bottom of each shot glass, a little more for cordials. Press down.

In a large mixing bowl, beat softened cream cheese and vanilla until fluffy. In another smaller microwavable mixing bowl, melt together milk and chocolate until melted and creamy. Add chocolate to cream cheese mixture, mix thoroughly. Gently fold in whipped topping. Fill each shot glass to the top with the chocolate mousse. I use my Dessert Pro filling tool with the star tip, which creates a wonderful swirl effect with the mousse. Garnish with a dollop of whipped topping, if desired. Finish off with a few shavings of chocolate or a chocolate wafer.

Serve and Enjoy !

This is one of those delicious chocolate and raspberry desserts that is very chocolatey and rich, but smooth as silk. This recipe makes 12 servings in small glass dessert dishes, 2-3 oz each.

CHOCOLATE RASPBERRY

Recipe

9 whole chocolate graham crackers or plain chocolate shortbread cookies (about a cup of coarse crumbs) 3 tbsp butter or margarine, melted, 2-3 tbsp honey.

2 cups (16 oz) whipping cream
12 oz semi-sweet chocolate chips
2 tbsp unsweetened cocoa powder
1/4 cup sugar
1 cup fresh raspberries or 1/2 cup raspberry jam

Crush graham crackers and mix with 3 tbsp butter and honey. Sometimes I just mix with lots of honey, without using butter. Divide equally in the bottom of the 12 small dishes, pack down firmly.

In a heavy saucepan, bring the whipping cream just to a boil, reduce heat to low and simmer 5 minutes, stirring constantly. Add chocolate chips, sugar and cocoa powder and mix until smooth and melted. Pour chocolate mixture into each dish over crust. Chill 1-2 hours or until firm.

Chocolate Raspberry can be served with fresh raspberries, raspberry puree or raspberry preserves on top.

Serve and Enjoy !

CHOCOLATE TIRAMISU

You don't get any more Italian than a delicious tiramisu dessert. I've added a little more chocolate to help put it over the edge.

This recipe is for those who don't have hours to spend in the kitchen preparing a traditional tiramisu. This is my quick and easy version. I think you'll like it.

Recipe

Ingredients:

1/3 cup sugar	1 cup strong coffee	8 oz whipped topping
2 tbsp rum	1 tbsp honey	1 tsp vanilla
1/4 cup milk	1/2 cup powdered sugar	4 oz semi-sweet chocolate, melted
1 pound cake	8 oz cream cheese, softened	

In a microwaveable bowl, add softened cream cheese, powdered sugar, milk, vanilla, 1 cup of whipped topping and melted chocolate. Mix well. Set aside. In another bowl, add the sugar, black coffee, rum and honey. Heat in a microwave until hot and mix well.

Place a slice of pound cake in the bottom of each glass bowl. Drizzle with a teaspoon of coffee rum sauce. Add a large spoonful of the chocolate cream mixture. Add another layer of cake, drizzle more coffee sauce and another spoonful of chocolate cream mixture. Finish off with a large dollop of whipped topping and some chocolate shavings.

Serve and Enjoy !

The more chocolate desserts I serve my family and friends, the more they want. So I'm guessing that this chocolate dessert will be a hit with your family as well.

This recipe will make enough to fill 10-12 shooters.

CHOCOLATE PARFAIT

Recipe
Ingredients:

2 small boxes of instant chocolate pudding
1 container of whipped topping
1 cup plain granola, optional
1/4 cup mini chocolate chips
4 cups cold milk, divided

Add a tablespoon of granola to the bottom of each mini parfait glass, saving about a 1/4 cup for garnish. In a large glass measuring cup or mixing bowl, add 2 cups cold milk and 1 box of chocolate pudding. Mix quickly with a whisk until it just starts to thicken. Pour immediately into each of the mini parfaits to about half full. Place in the refrigerator while you prepare the next step.

In the same large glass measuring cup, add another 2 cups of cold milk and the second box of chocolate pudding. Mix immediately until it just starts to set. Then add about 2 cups whipped topping. Beat until smooth. Quickly pour into each of the mini parfaits. Top off with some granola or whipped topping and mini chocolate chips. Refrigerate for about an hour or so.

Serve and Enjoy !

Holiday
Buffet
Dinner

Honey Orange Glazed Ham

Baking a ham is a rather simple process. Simple for some, more difficult for others. The simple baking rule should always be, heat for 15 minutes for every pound. I always cover the ham with foil for half the time and then uncover it for the rest. The real pizzazz is in the glaze.

Below are four of my favorite glazes that are all simple to prepare and will add the extra zing you are looking for to impress your guests.

Recipes

Smokey Bacon Glaze - 1 c brown sugar, 1/2 c pineapple juice and 1/2 c honey and 1/4 c crumbled cooked bacon. Mix in a large microwaveable measuring cup and heat slightly until melted. Let cool slightly.

Honey Orange Glaze - 1 c brown sugar, 1/2 c orange or pineapple juice and 1/2 c honey or 1/2 c maple syrup. Mix in a large microwaveable measuring cup and heat slightly until melted. Let cool slightly.

Cranberry Glaze - 1-1/2 c cranberry sauce, 1/2 c brown sugar, 1/3 c red wine, 1 tsp mustard, 1 tbsp grated orange zest. Put everything together in a saucepan and heat almost to a boil. Let cool slightly.

Honey Mustard Glaze - 1 c brown sugar, 1/4 c dijon mustard and 1/2 c honey. Mix in a large microwaveable measuring cup and heat slightly until melted. Let cool slightly.

All glazes are applied every 30 minutes while baking and every 10 minutes the last 30 minutes. You'll even have some extra in a bowl for those who want some for dipping or as a condiment.

The original salad from the Waldorf_Astoria Hotel in New York City, my mother has been making this wonderful salad for our family for years. It used to be a Thanksgiving tradition that has now carried over to the Christmas holidays. She gave me this recipe when she wanted someone else in the family to make it for all our family dinners.

Waldorf Salad

Recipe

Here is what you will need:

4-5 crisp apples, cored and cubed
1/2 cup chopped pecans or walnuts
1 cup mayo
1/4 cup whipped topping, optional

4-5 stalks of celery, coarsely chopped
2 cups seedless grapes, cut lengthwise
1/4 cup sugar

In a large mixing bowl, combine the mayo and sugar. Mix well. Add the apples, pecans, celery and grapes and toss until well coated. Add the whipped topping if you want it a little sweeter. I have been known to add a 1/4 cup dried cherries or craisins, but my mother will have no part of this version! Most of the rest of the family thinks it is ok. Refrigerate until ready to serve.

Enjoy !

Margaret's Deviled Eggs

Margaret Deedman has been making these devilled eggs for almost every family function since I can remember. They have always been a family favorite and are usually gone before dinner is even served. So here is her famous recipe. We hope you enjoy it as much as my family has over the years.

Recipe

Here is what you will need to prepare:

1 dozen hard boiled eggs
1/2 cup regular or spicy mustard
1/4 cup mayo
several olives (8-9), sliced for garnish
dash of paprika
salt and pepper

Cooking hard boiled eggs is not difficult, but there is a trick to it. Start with cold water and bring eggs to a boil. Turn heat down to a simmer and cook for another 10-12 minutes. Immediately run under cold water.

Peel the eggs and cut in half horizonally. Remove the yolks and mash in a small mixing bowl. Add the mayo and mustard and mix well. Fill each egg cavity with mixture. Sprinkle with paprika and garnish with a slice of an olive and salt and pepper.
Refrigerate until ready to serve.

Enjoy !

We have been making these cheesy potatoes in my family for years. They are perfect for a family buffet. What I really like is that they can be made the day before and baked when needed.

There are many variations. I'll give you the basic one with an added option.

Cheesy Potatoes

Recipe

Here is what you will need to get started:

One bag frozen hash brown potatoes, thawed
1 pkg cheddar cheese, shredded
1 can of any cream soup
1/4 cup chopped green onions
1/4 cup green pepper, chopped
1/2 cup melted butter
2 cups plain corn flakes

Another option: add 1/2 cup crumbled cooked bacon

In a large mixing bowl,
add the hash brown potatoes,
shredded cheese, onions,
green peppers and cream soup.
Mix well. Pour or spoon
into the large 9x13 casserole.
In the same mixing bowl,
add the corn flakes and
melted butter, mix well.
Pour over the potatoes mixture
and spread around to cover.

Bake at 350 degrees for one
hour or until heated through.

Serve and Enjoy !

Mixed Veggie Medley

I borrowed this recipe from a good friend of mine, Sue Beckert. It has always been a great side dish at many of our family dinners and can be made the day before if needed.

Preheat oven to 350 degrees

Recipe

Ingredients:

1 large bag of frozen mixed vegetables, thawed slightly
1 cup sour cream
1 can cream of celery soup

1 can of sliced water chestnuts
1 cup shredded swiss cheese
1 can of fried onion rings

Mix everything (except the onion rings) together in a 9x13 baking dish. Crush the onion rings in your hands and sprinkle over the entire casserole. Bake in the oven for 30-40 minutes or until heated through.
Serve immediately.

Enjoy !

These mini pies are perfect for the holidays or any buffet setting or tasting party. I always make several different versions to please each of my guests.

All of the different pie fillings can be purchased at your local grocery store.

Preheat the oven to 350 degrees.

This will make 24 mini pies.

Recipe

You will need 2 twelve section muffin pans

two packages of pre-made pie crusts, at room temperature
1/4 cup butter or margarine, softened
1/4 cup flour

Several different types of pie fillings. I usually choose a small can of cherry, apple, peach, strawberry-rhubarb and lemon. These will cover most of your guests' taste buds. If you really want to go all out, get a box of chocolate pudding (the cooked version)

Roll out or unfold the pie crusts. Spread each crust with about a tablespoon of butter and lightly dust with flour. Do that to the other side as well. Take a round cookie cutter or an empty soup can will work as well, about an 1" larger then the bottom diameter of the muffin pan and cut out round pie discs. Place in the bottom of each muffin pan cavity and form a pie crust about a 1/2" deep. Poke with a fork on the bottom and sides. Bake for 20 minutes until light brown. Remove from oven and let cool. Fill with your various different pie fillings and bake again if required for about 20 minutes or until hot. Let cool. Carefully remove from pan and serve.

Enjoy !

Thanksgiving and Fall Harvest

Mashed Potato Casserole

This is another perfect side dish for any pot luck or family buffet. We usually make one plain and one with garlic and bacon. Both are equally delicious.

Preheat oven to 350 degrees.

Recipe

You will need one 9x13 baking dish and the following ingredients:

6 cups instant mashed potatoes
1 cup of chicken broth or stock
1 pkg ranch dressing or 1/4 cup liquid
1/4 cup finely chopped onions

2 cans evaporated milk
4 cups hot water
2 cups corn flakes
1/4 cup parmesan cheese

1 stick of butter
1 cup sour cream
4 tbsp melted butter
salt & pepper to taste

In a large mixing bowl, combine the very hot water, stick of butter, chicken stock, sour cream and evaporated milk. Mix well. Add the chopped onions, powder or liquid ranch dressing and any additional ingredients you want and mix again. Fold in the instant mashed potatoes. Mix well. Spoon into a 9x13 baking dish coated with cooking spray and smooth mixture out. In the same mixing bowl combine the corn flakes and 4 tbsp melted butter. Toss until well coated. Sprinkle over the potatoes mixture as evenly as possible. Sprinkle with parmesan cheese and bake for about 40-45 minutes.

Serve hot and Enjoy !

Nothing is more flavorful and delicious than a fresh roasted turkey. Whether it is Thanksgiving, Christmas or just a plain old family buffet, roasted turkey is perfect.

I have always used a cooking bag and my turkeys always come out brown and delicious with lots of juice for gravy.

Preheat oven to 350 degrees.

Roasted Turkey

Recipe

The cooking bag box will tell you how long to cook your turkey and it depends on how much it weighs. I always add an additional 30 minutes and it will be just as moist and perfectly cooked.

You will need one turkey size cooking bag, 3 tbsp flour, several stalks of celery, 2 onions, 2 carrots, one teaspoon of Italian seasoning, optional and 1 cup water.

Follow the directions on the cooking bag box. Cut up the celery, carrots and onion and put about half inside the turkey cavity and the remaining around the outside of the turkey but still inside the bag. Add one cup of water inside the cavity. Seal the cooking bag and place in a large roasting pan and bake accordingly. When finished cooking, let stand about 15 minutes. Cut a small hole in the corner of the cooking bag and carefully hold the turkey and roasting pan with thick hot pads and pour the liquid into a large saucepan. This makes the best turkey gravy you have ever tasted. Remove the turkey from the cooking bag and let rest another 15-20 minutes while you make the gravy. Place on a large platter and garnish with sliced oranges and apples.

Serve and Enjoy !

Sweet Potato Casserole

Nothing is better in the fall or for Thanksgiving dinner than a hot dish of sweet potatoes. It's very easy to prepare and equally as delicious.

Recipe

This is what you will need:

- 2 large cans of sweet potatoes or yams
- 1 cup dark brown sugar, divided
- 1/2 cup chopped pecans

- 1/4 cup milk or half & half
- 1 stick of melted butter, divided
- 2 tbsp maple syrup

In a large microwaveable bowl, place the drained yams cut into small pieces. Microwave for about 3-4 minutes until hot. Mash with a potato masher or wooden spoon. Add the milk, half the melted butter and 1/2 cup dark brown sugar. Mix well. Pour into a small casserole. Smooth out the surface.

In a small microwaveable measuring cup, add 1/2 cup dark brown sugar, melted butter and maple syrup. Mix well. Microwave for a minute or two until smooth. You may need to add a few drops of water. Stir in the finely chopped pecans. Spoon over the top of the sweet potatoes. Bake in the oven for 45 minutes or in the microwave for about 6-7 minutes or until hot. Let stand a few minutes before serving.

Enjoy !

This classic stuffing is a perfect side dish. There are many variations to making this, but this is my classic one.

Classic Dressing

Recipe
Ingredients:

1 large bag of stuffing mix or 7-8 slices of dark toasted bread, cut into small pieces
1 can of chicken stock or broth
1 cup of chopped celery
1 carrot, finely chopped
1 apple, cored and finely chopped
1/4 cup chopped pecans
1 stick of butter or margarine, melted

In a large mixing bowl, mix all the dry ingredients. Add the chicken stock and mix well. Add the melted butter and mix again. Pour into a large baking dish and cover with aluminum foil. Bake for 45 minutes at 350 degrees. Remove foil and bake another 15 minutes until golden brown.

Serve and Enjoy !

Cranberry Salad

My family makes cranberry salad for almost every occasion. This one is pretty quick, easy and very tasty.

Recipe

Here is what you will need:

2 - 14oz cans of cranberry sauce
rind from one orange, finely chopped
one large crisp apple, cored and chopped
3-4 stalks of celery, chopped
1 small can of crushed pineapple, drained
1/4 cup pecans, chopped

Just mix everything together in a large mixing bowl and that's it. Pour mixture into either a fancy glass serving bowl or into individual dishes, depending on the occasion. Refrigerate until ready to serve.

Enjoy !

Scalloped corn traces its roots back to the days of the pilgrims. It is a creamy and delicious casserole and another perfect compliment to turkey, chicken or any wild game bird.

Preheat oven to 350 degrees

Scalloped Corn

Recipe

Here is what you will need:

1 large bag of frozen whole kernel corn or 2 cans
1/2 green pepper, chopped
several green onions, chopped
1 egg
one box of Jiffy corn bread mix
1 cup milk
4 tbsp of melted butter or margarine
1 cup sour cream
1 cup bread crumbs or french onion rings, optional for topping

In a large mixing bowl, add the corn, green pepper and green onion. Mix well. Mix in the corn bread mix. In another small bowl, mix together the milk, egg, sour cream and melted butter. Combine the two mixtures together and mix well. Pour or spoon into a casserole dish sprayed with cooking spray. Sprinkle the top with bread crumbs or french onion rings. Bake uncovered for 60 minutes and golden brown.

Serve and Enjoy !

Green Bean Casserole

A green bean casserole is almost as famous with a Thanksgiving dinner as the roasted turkey itself. My family serves it at almost every family get together. There are probably many different versions, but here is mine.

Preheat oven to 350 degrees

Recipe

Ingredients:

1 - 25oz bag of frozen green beans, thawed
1 can of cream of mushroom soup
1 can of fried onion rings, divided

1/2 cup milk
1 tbsp worcestershire sauce
salt & pepper

This recipe works well with either french style or fresh green beans.

Add the green beans, mushroom soup, milk and worcestershire sauce in a large mixing bowl or just put it all into your casserole dish. Mix well. Salt and pepper to taste. Mix in half the crumbled onion rings. Sprinkle the remaining onion rings on the top. Bake at 350 degrees for about 45 minutes or until hot.

Serve and Enjoy !

I borrowed this recipe from an old friend years ago. I usually refer to this as my holiday pudding because tomato pudding scares most people away, especially the kids. It may be made with tomatoes, but you would never know it. It has a deliciously sweet taste that is perfect with turkey or ham.

Preheat oven to 350 degrees

Tomato Pudding

Recipe

Here is what you will need:

6 slices of very dark toast, almost burnt
1 large can of stewed tomatoes
1 stick of butter, melted
3 tbsp flour
2 cups of dark brown sugar
pinch of salt

Cut the burnt toast into 1/2" pieces, crust and all. In a large mixing bowl, add the stewed tomatoes, brown sugar, flour, salt and melted butter. Mix well. Fold in the toast pieces and mix until well coated. Pour into a small casserole and bake uncovered at 350 degrees for an hour. This can be served hot or at room temperature.

Serve and Enjoy !

Fourth of July
Celebration

Fireworks Punch

This is one of my favorite punches. You can use almost any liquor to add the zing, so I've used them all. When we are sitting on the patio watching the fireworks over the lake, this punch just hits the spot on those warm summer nights. But be careful, because it will sneak up on you.

Recipe

Ingredients:

1 cup vodka
1 cup gin
1 cup tequila
1 cup light rum
1/2 cup cream de menthe
1 cup fresh lemon juice
1-2 liters lemon-lime soda
1 - 16oz can of cola
1/2 simple syrup
lots of ice

2 lemons, 2 oranges and 2 limes, sliced

In a large glass punch bowl, carefully add all the ingredients except the ice. Mix together and let sit for 30 minutes. When your guests arrive, add the ice and the sliced lemons, limes and oranges.

You can add as much lemon-lime soda as you want. The less you use the stronger the punch.

Serve and Enjoy !

The perfect BBQ is all about the sauce. Some like it smokey and hot, while others like it sweet. This recipe is a combination of both, but you can adjust it either way.

BBQ Beef or Pork

Recipe
Ingredients:

3-4 lb beef or pork roast
3 tbsp worcestershire sauce
1/2 cup dark brown sugar
1/2 cup soy sauce
2 cloves of garlic, crushed
1 tsp crushed red pepper

In a small mixing bowl, add all the ingredients except the meat, mix well. In a large Dutch oven, add the meat and pour the sauce mixture over the meat. Bake for about 2-3 hours until it is very tender. Let cool.

For the BBQ sauce, you'll need: 3 cups tomato sauce, 1 cup apple vinegar, 1 cup worcestershire sauce, 1 cup dark brown sugar, 1/4 cup bacon bits and 1 tbsp dijon mustard. Mix everything together in a heavy saucepan. Bring to boil and then reduce heat to a simmer, stirring occasionally until it thickens, about 30 minutes.

Shred the beef or pork roast and add the BBQ sauce. Mix well. Can be served hot or cold.

Enjoy !

Mixed Fruit Salad

Nothing is more refreshing than a bowl of fresh fruit. No matter what time of year, fresh fruit just hits the spot. It is also a nice side dish for those who are more health conscious. So I've given you the option to use whipped topping or vanilla yogurt. Both work and taste delicious.

Recipe

Here is what you will need:

- 2 cups fresh pineapple, chunked
- 2 cups cantaloupe, chunked
- 2 cups fresh strawberries, sliced
- 2 cups fresh blueberries
- 2 cups fresh blackberries
- 2 cups fresh honey dew melon, chunked
- 2 cups fresh raspberries
- 2 cups whipped topping or vanilla yogurt

Mix everything together in a large mixing bowl. Carefully fold in the whipped topping or vanilla yogurt, or serve on the side as a topping. Pour carefully into a glass serving bowl or footed trifle bowl. Refrigerate until ready to serve.

Enjoy !

Nothing says summer or the Fourth of July like fresh homemade potato salad. The key here is in the mustard, which adds the right amount of zip to the rather plain mayonnaise. The more you use, the more zip !

Potato or Macaroni Salad

Recipe

Here is what you will need:

7-8 large potatoes, peeled and cooked or
1 lb cooked spiral macaroni

1 cup celery, chopped
2 carrots, peeled and chopped
1 cup mayonnaise
4 eggs, hard boiled and chopped
pinch of celery salt
1/4 cup spicy or regular mustard
salt & pepper
paprika for garnish
1 onion, chopped or
1-2 small green onions, chopped

In a small mixing bowl, add the mayo, mustard and celery salt. Mix well. In a large mixing bowl, add the cooled cubed potatoes (or cooked macaroni), chopped celery, onions, carrots and eggs. Mix this up well. Add the mayo mixture and toss together until well coated. Salt and pepper to taste. Transfer to a beautiful glass serving bowl and sprinkle lightly with paprika. Refrigerate until ready to serve.

Enjoy !

St. Patrick's Day Party Buffet

Shamrock Punch

A traditional St. Paddy's day party would not be the same without some kind of green beverage. Some definitely prefer a green beer, but for those who want to serve a big group, this is the perfect party punch to help celebrate the big green day.

Recipe

Here is what you will need:

- 2 cans frozen limeade
- 1 pkg lime jello
- 2 liters of lemon-lime soda
- 1 empty limeade can of tequila
- 2-3 limes, sliced

In a large glass punch bowl, carefully add the frozen limeade and soda. Mix until limeade is dissolved. Stir in the lime jello and tequila. Add some ice to chill and lime slices for garnish. Serve with a bright green cocktail napkin and Enjoy !

Nothing is more traditional for a St. Patrick's Day party or get together than corned beef and cabbage or as the Irish called it: Jiggs Dinner. It takes a little time to cook but is a pretty easy recipe to prepare.

Corned Beef & Cabbage

Recipe

Here is what you will need:

3 lbs of corned beef or a large chunk of ham
8-10 carrots, peeled and chunked
pinch of celery salt and fennel

1 large head of cabbage, quartered
5-6 potatoes, peeled and quartered
2 bay leaves
salt and pepper

In a large stock pot, place the corned beef or ham and cover with water. Season with celery salt, bay leaves and fennel. Cook over medium heat for about 2 hours. Now add all the vegetables and cook another hour or so until the vegetables are tender. Remove from pot and place on a large platter or casserole for serving. Sprinkle with salt and pepper to taste and serve.

Enjoy !

Shamrock Cookies

Everyone loves sugar cookies, especially when they are shaped like shamrocks to help celebrate St. Paddy's Day.

This recipe will make about 36 cookies.

Recipe

Here is what you will need for the cookies:

1/3 cup butter or margarine
1/3 cup shortening
3/4 cup sugar
1 tsp baking powder
1 egg
1 tsp vanilla
2 cups flour
pinch of salt
green sugar sprinkles

In a mixing bowl, beat the butter and shortening for about a minute. Add the sugar, baking powder and salt. Mix well. Beat in vanilla and egg. Start adding all the flour a little at a time. Mix well. Divide in half, wrap in wax paper and chill for 3 hours in the refrigerator.

On a lightly floured surface, roll out each package of chilled dough about 1/4" thick. With a lightly floured shamrock shape cookie cutter or a plain round one, cut out the shape. Place on an ungreased cookie sheet. Bake at 375 degrees for about 7 minutes until edges are firm and lightly browned on the bottom. Cool on a rack.

Frost with your favorite vanilla frosting tinted with green food coloring and sprinkle with green sugar sprinkles.

Serve and Enjoy !

This is one of our family favorites and we serve it almost anytime of the year. It is perfect served with corned beef and cabbage, since not everyone likes corned beef, this is a nice alternative and a great vegetarian dish.

For something a little different, try adding 1/4 cup bacon bits and or 1/2 cup chopped tomatoes or green pepper.

Preheat oven to 350 degrees.

Five Cheese Mac'n Cheese

Recipe

Here is what you will need:

1 lb penne pasta, cooked according to package
1/2 cup fontina cheese, shredded
1/2 cup gorgonzola cheese, shredded
1/2 cup mozzarella cheese, shredded
1/4 cup butter or margarine
1 tsp parsley flakes and dried basil

2 cans evaporated milk
3/4 cup parmesan cheese, shredded
1/2 cup cheddar cheese, shredded
3/4 cup white wine
1/4 cup flour
salt and pepper

In a heavy duty saucepan, melt the butter. Add the flour and cook one minute to make a rue. Stir constantly. Add the milk a little at a time and then the white wine. Bring to a boil, stirring constantly until it thickens. Reduce heat and add all the shredded cheeses, parsley and basil. Mix well. In a large baking dish, add the pasta and then pour in the cheese mixture. Mix well. Bake for 30 minutes until hot and golden brown.

Serve and Enjoy !

Halloween
Ghosts & Goblins

SLOPPY JOES

Sloppy Joes, potato chips and pickles are all you'll ever need for a great lunch or light dinner. It's the perfect dinner for when you are passing out candy to all those darling little witches and goblins. I make a couple of platters and have them ready for all my guests who drop in unexpectedly.

Recipe

Ingredients:

2-3 lbs of ground chuck	1 can tomato sauce	1 onion, finely chopped
1 green pepper, finely chopped	1/4 cup brown sugar	pinch of garlic salt

In a large skillet, brown the ground beef with the chopped onion on medium heat. Drain off the grease and pat with a piece of paper towel. Add the tomato sauce, brown sugar, green pepper and garlic salt. Heat for about 30 minutes on medium heat. Serve from the skillet or pour into a casserole dish for serving. Serve on hamburger or hot dog buns.

Enjoy !

I like to add a little rum to this punch, but if you are having children around for the party, I'd omit it completely.

WITCH'S BATS & BREW

Recipe
Ingredients:

1 gallon apple cider
1 cup orange juice
1 apple, cored and sliced
1 orange, sliced
1 tsp cinnamon
pinch of nutmeg and cloves
1 tbsp sugar, optional
one cup rum, optional
several cups of ice, cubes or crushed

Carefully pour the apple cider into the glass jug or punch bowl. Add the orange juice and rum. Stir. Add the orange and apple slices and all the spices. Stir and leave at room temperature. When ready to serve, add the ice.

Serve and Enjoy !

HOMEMADE CARAMEL CORN

I borrowed this recipe from an associate of mine, Joe Mefferd. He has been making it for his family for years. It makes an ideal snack for all those little munchkins, young and old, on Halloween night.

Recipe
Ingredients:

- 4 quarts popped popcorn, removed unpopped kernels
- 2 sticks of butter or margarine
- 1 cup dark brown sugar
- 1/2 cup light corn syrup
- 1 tsp baking soda
- 1/2 tsp salt

Place the popped corn in a very large mixing bowl. Set aside.

In a large pan, melt the butter on medium heat. Add the dark brown sugar, corn syrup and salt. Mix well. Bring to a boil making sure that you have incorporated all of the ingredients. Add the baking soda. The mixture will multiply in volume. Pour the caramel mixture over the popcorn and mix well to coat all the corn. Spread mixture on two cookies sheets that have been sprayed with cooking spray. Place in the oven at 200 degrees for one hour. Rotate the cookie sheet every 15 minutes. Let cool and break into pieces.

Serve and Enjoy !

Pumpkin Creams

This is a perfect little dessert along with a warm cup of coffee or a glass of Witch's Brew. Your guests will love the smooth creamy taste of pumpkin.

Recipe

Ingredients:

2 - 8oz pkg cream cheese
1 cup canned pumpkin
1/2 cup heavy cream, divided

1 - 8 oz container of whipped topping
1 cup graham cracker crumbs
1/2 stick butter or margarine, melted

1 tsp vanilla
1/2 cup sugar, divided

In a small mixing bowl, add the cracker crumbs, 1/4 cup sugar and melted butter. Mix well. Fill the bottom of each dessert dish with a thin layer of cracker mixture.

In a large mixing bowl, add 1 package softened cream cheese, 1 cup pumpkin, 1/4 cup sugar and 1/4 cup heavy cream. Mix well. Add 8 oz whipped topping and mix again. Fill each dessert dish to about half full with this pumpkin mixture. Tap down to flatten and refrigerate.

In another mixing bowl, add 8 oz cream cheese, softened and 1/4 cup heavy cream. Mix well. Fold in the whipped topping. Cover the pumpkin with the cream mixture. Refrigerate an hour or so. Serve at room temperature.

Serve and Enjoy !

New Year's Eve
Celebration

Champagne Party Punch

A champagne punch is perfect when you want to celebrate something special. It's ideal for a wedding brunch, New Year's celebration or any special occasion.

An inexpensive champagne is fine, since you are going to dilute it with soda.

Using regular white wine will also work, but somehow it does not have the same panache as champagne.

Recipe

64 oz club soda or lemon-lime soda
2 bottles chilled champagne
1 orange, sliced for garnish
4 cups of ice cubes

Large pieces of glass are somewhat fragile and should be handled carefully, especially when washing. Do not shock them in either too hot or too cold of water. This can cause them to crack or break.

In a large punch bowl, carefully add the club soda and chilled champagne. Add the ice and orange slices and you are all ready to enjoy the festivities.

Serve and Enjoy !

Broiled pork tenderloin is one of my real favorites when it comes to entertaining. It is relatively inexpensive and really looks marvelous and tastes delicious when served on a buffet table.

Broiled Pork Tenderloin

Recipe

Here is what you will need:

2 pork tenderloins, 3/4 - 1 lb each	4 tbsp soy sauce
2 tbsp olive oil	1 tsp ground ginger
1-2 garlic cloves, crushed	2 tsp dark brown sugar or honey
2 tbsp dijon mustard	1/2 tsp fresh ground pepper

Combine everything except the pork in a mixing bowl. Mix well. The pork tenderloin will cook faster if you butterfly it lengthwise. Place the pork tenderloin in a 9x13 baking dish. Pour about half the marinade mixture over the pork and into the cavity of the tenderloin. Let marinate for a couple of hours, turning pork occasionally. Keep the remaining marinade to use during the cooking.

Grill or broil in the oven for about 20 minutes or until very golden brown. I turn the tenderloin every 5 minutes or so. Baste with the reserve marinade. Let stand a few minutes before cutting into angled pieces for serving. Pour any left over marinade over the pork right before you serve it.

Enjoy !

Tuscan Flatbread

A classic flatbread is absolutely perfect for any special occasion. It's relatively easy to prepare and can be adapted or adjusted to almost any flavor or toppings you want to serve.

Preheat oven to 425 degrees

Recipe

1 can classic refrigerated pizza dough
1 tbsp olive oil
1 tsp dried basil
1 tsp dried rosemary, crushed
1/2 tsp minced garlic
pinch of sea salt
2 small ripe tomatoes, thinely sliced
1/2 cup fresh shredded parmesan cheese

Spray a cookie sheet with cooking spray. Place the store bought pizza dough on the cookie sheet and spread out as thin as you can to form a large rectangle. Brush the dough with olive oil and sprinkle generously with dried basil and rosemary. Add a pinch of salt. Add the thinly sliced tomatoes. Bake in oven at 425 degrees for 8-9 minutes until golden brown. Remove from oven and sprinkle lightly with parmesan cheese. Bake for another 3-4 minutes until cheese is melted and crust is a dark golden brown. (Flatbread is suppose to be a little overcooked or crispy.) Cut into squares.

Serve and Enjoy !

I borrowed this wonderful appetizer recipe from a family member, Carol Luscombe. She recently brought it to one of our family get togethers and it was an instant hit. I hope you enjoy it as much as we did.

Pesto Spread

Recipe

1 - 8oz pkg cream cheese, softened
4 - 6 oz pesto sauce
1/2 cup chopped pecans or walnuts
1/2 cup chopped black olives
various plain crackers

Place the softened block of cream cheese on a rectangle plate. Pour the pesto sauce over the cream cheese. Sprinkle the chopped nuts and chopped black olives over the pesto sauce. Arrange some plain crackers around the server and you are ready to go. Very easy to prepare but really delicious.

Serve and Enjoy !

Italian Caprese Salad

In August when the cherry tomatoes are at their peak, nothing is more wonderful than a fresh Caprese Salad. Your guests will love it.

Recipe

Here is what you will need:

2 cups cherry tomatoes, sliced the long way
8 - 12 oz fresh mozzarella cheese, cubed
1 can of sliced black olives
about a cup of fresh chopped basil
some balsamic vinegar and olive oil
fresh ground pepper

In a large glass serving bowl, place the first 4 ingredients and toss together. Sprinkle with balsamic vinegar, olive oil and fresh ground pepper. Refrigerate until ready to use. Serve at room temperature.

Enjoy !

This relatively healthy dessert is almost perfect anytime. It is light and creamy and will make enough for your whole family and more.

Fruit & Cream

Recipe

Here is what you will need:

1 angel food cake
2 cups fresh strawberries, sliced
3-4 fresh kiwis, peeled and sliced
2 cups blueberries
2 cups fresh raspberries
3-4 sliced bananas
2 cups fresh blackberries
24 oz whipped topping

Cut the angel food cake into bite size pieces. Line the outside of the trifle bowl with strawberries. Fill in the center of your trifle bowl with some cake to hold the strawberries in place. Add a layer of all the fruit you are using. Cover with whipped topping. Add a ring of kiwi just like the strawberries and more cake and fruit to hold that in place, and another layer of whipped topping. Fill remaining bowl with cake, fruit and top off with whipped topping. Garnish the top with a ring of fruit in some sort of pattern or design. Refrigerate for about an hour.

Serve and Enjoy !

Healthy Options
Cocktail Buffet

Salsa Chicken Casserole

This is another one of those rather healthy casseroles that can be made ahead of time and popped in the oven right before your guests arrive. I've made it in individual casseroles for a dinner party or a large casserole for a buffet. Both ways are delicious and healthy.

Preheat oven to 350 degrees.

Recipe

Ingredients:

2 grilled boneless chicken breasts
1-1/2 cups salsa
1 onion, chopped
1 cup frozen peas
2-3 tomatoes, chopped

2 sweet potatoes, peeled and thinly sliced
1 can of black beans, drained
1 cup frozen corn
1/2 cup sliced almonds

In a large skillet, add the sliced sweet potatoes and salsa and saute for 5 minutes. Cut the grilled chicken breasts diagonally into bite size pieces. In a 9x13 casserole dish add all the ingredients and toss together. Add a little more salsa to moisten if necessary. Bake in moderate oven at 350 degrees for about 30 minutes.

Serve and Enjoy !

This tropical smoothie has a unique flavor of fresh mango. Orange and pineapple have been around for ages, but mangos are relatively new to everyday consumers. So adding fresh pineapple and orange juice will help boost this mango smoothie to another level for a high energy drink. Try it and you'll be pleasantly surprised at the unique flavor it delivers. Be sure the mangos are ripe (they will feel kind of soft).

Tropical Smoothies

Recipe

Here is what you will need:

This recipe will make 3-4 smoothies in a tall soda glass.

1 cup orange mango juice
2 ripe mangos, peeled, pitted and diced
2 cups fresh pineapple
2 cups peaches, sliced
1 cup crushed ice
2 cups vanilla yogurt, plain yogurt or low-fat cottage cheese

In a blender, add the orange mango juice, pineapple, peaches, crushed ice and the fresh mango pieces. Blend well. Add the yogurt or cottage cheese and blend until smooth. Serve in very tall, skinny soda glass.

Enjoy !

Fruit Infused Iced Tea

Fruit infused water and iced teas are a perfect thirst quencher when you need to cool down and want to stay away from all the calories or carbohydrates.

Making it in a large pitcher is perfect for serving something delicious to all your health conscious guests.

Recipe

Ingredients:

4-5 tea bags or a pouch of loose tea, basic orange pekoe

2 cups of fresh fruit (strawberries, raspberries, sliced peaches, mango, etc.)

1/2 cup honey, optional
2 quarts water
lots of ice for serving

Bring the water to boil in a large saucepan, add the tea bags, remove from heat. Let cool for a few minutes and add the fresh fruit and let steep for about an hour. Remove the tea bags and fruit. Add some honey if you want it a little sweeter. Pour into a large pitcher or container and refrigerate. Serve in tall glasses with plenty of ice.

Enjoy !

Kabobs is a perfect appetizer for a healthy buffet party. Grilled chicken or shrimp along with some fresh vegetables makes the perfect snack for all your party guests.

Chicken & Veggie Kabobs

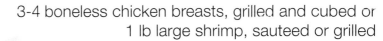

Recipe
Ingredients:

3-4 boneless chicken breasts, grilled and cubed or
1 lb large shrimp, sauteed or grilled

2 green peppers, chunked
1 onion, peeled and chunked
10-12 whole mushrooms, sliced
2 cups, about 30 cherry tomatoes
15-20 - 5" wooden skewers
balsamic vinegar

Take a wooden skewer and place one piece of chicken, mushroom, green pepper, onion and cherry tomato in no particular order onto the skewer. Drizzle with balsamic vinegar or non-fat Italian dressing. Arrange on a tiered server or serving plate.

Serve and Enjoy !

Turkey Casserole

When having a cocktail party with your friends, nothing is more special than having something that is really good and healthy to eat. Save the carbs and calories for a cocktail or two.

Preheat oven to 350 degrees.

Recipe

Ingredients:

1 cup canned navy beans
1 tsp coriander
1-1/2 lb ground turkey
1/2 cup sliced almonds
1-1/2 cups low-fat white cheddar cheese , shredded

1 cup milk
1 tsp salt
1 cup sweet onion, chopped
2 cups asparagus, 1" pieces

1 tsp tumeric
1 cup vegetable stock
2 cups sliced carrots
2 cups grated cabbage
cooking spray

In a mixing bowl, add the navy beans, 1/4 cup milk, tumeric, coriander, salt and mash together. Add the rest of the milk and vegetable stock and mix well. Spray a skillet with cooking spray and saute the ground turkey in batches, if needed, until fully cooked. Transfer to a large casserole, add the remaining vegetables, shredded cheese and almonds. Toss with the bean mixture until well coated. Bake in oven for 30 minutes.

Serve and Enjoy !

Pesto Pizza

Pizza is synonymous with people and parties. This recipe, when served on a whole wheat tortilla, makes it all the more rewarding and nutritious when it comes to eating healthy.

Almost any fresh seasonal vegetable will work as a topping on this pizza.

Preheat oven to 400 degrees

Recipe

Here is what you will need to make 4 - 8" pizzas.

2 grilled chicken breasts
2-3 whole wheat tortillas
1/4 cup pesto, 6oz jar
1/2 cup broccoli florets, chopped
fresh or sundried tomatoes
1/2 cup asparagus, sliced

1 cup white cheddar, mozzarella, feta or havarti cheese, shredded

Lightly coat a cookie sheet with some cooking spray. Place the tortilla shell on the tray. Spread the pesto thinly over the surface of the tortilla shell to about 1/2" from the edge. Spread the broccoli, asparagus and tomatoes evenly over the entire pesto surface of the tortilla shell. Top off with the shredded cheese of your choice. Bake until cheese is melted and tortilla shell lightly browned, about 10 minutes. Cut into small 2' squares for serving.

Serve and Enjoy !

Baby or Bridal Shower

Sherbet Punch

Serving a punch at any baby shower or bridal shower is about as traditional as it gets. Some of the gals like to jazz it up a little by adding a little vodka or white wine to help them celebrate this special occasion.

Here is what you will need to make a very festive punch.

Recipe

2 - 2 liter ginger ale or lemon-lime soda
2 cups cranberry juice or orange juice
1 quart sherbet, any flavor
several oranges, sliced
one ice ring or lots of ice cubes

Punch bowls or any large pieces of glass are somewhat fragile and should be handled carefully, especially when washing. Do not shock them in either too hot or too cold of water. This can cause them to crack or break.

To make an ice ring, take a 12" diameter ring pan and fill it with water along with some orange slices or fresh strawberries, raspberries, etc. Freeze overnight until solid.

Carefully pour the ginger ale and cranberry juice into the punch bowl. Add the sherbet and stir slightly. Carefully add the ice ring and garnish with the orange slices.

Serve and Enjoy !

Small tea sandwiches are just perfect for any get together when you want something to be a little more petite or delicate looking than a big sandwich. These are perfect for showers, brunches or afternoon teas.

Tea Sandwiches

Recipe

Here is what you will need:

1 lb chicken salad
1 lb tuna salad
1 lb egg salad
1 cucumber, sliced
4 oz pkg cream cheese
1 tsp dill weed
1 loaf of thin sliced wheat or rye bread

Take a slice of bread and cover with either chicken, tuna or egg salad. Cover with another slice of bread. With a very sharp serrated knife, cut away the outside crust and then either cut into quarters, squares or triangle shapes.

For the cucumber sandwiches, remove the crusts and then cut your bread into squares. Cover each square with cream creese, a slice of cucumber and sprinkle with dill weed. You can leave open face or cover with another square of bread.

Arrange on a platter with a small dish of olives.

Serve and Enjoy !

Mini Quiches

The mini quiches are a perfect compliment to the tea sandwiches. These small bite size appetizers are ideal when you want just a little bite of something.

Preheat oven to 350 degrees

Recipe

Ingredients:

1 pkg refrigerator pie crusts
8 slices of cooked bacon, crumbled
4 oz shredded swiss cheese
2 tbsp butter or margarine
4 eggs, beaten
1/4 cup chopped green onion
1 tsp salt
1/2 cup flour
1-1/2 cups milk
1 muffin pan

Unroll the pie crusts and lightly flour each side. Using a round cookie cutter, cut out round pieces of crust about an inch larger that the bottom of the muffin tin. Press crust into the bottom of each opening. Add about a heaping spoonful of crumbled bacon and shredded cheese.

Combine beaten eggs, butter, onion, flour, salt and milk in a mixing bowl. Whisk together until smooth. Pour enough into each to fill almost full. Bake in preheated oven for about 30 minutes until slightly golden brown around the edges. Remove from oven. Serve hot or room temperature.

Enjoy !

This is the perfect dessert that is light and refreshing and looks as good as it tastes. Served on a footed server or tray makes them look all the more special.

Pudding Parfaits

Recipe

Here is what you will need:

1 box of instant chocolate pudding
1 box of lemon instant pudding
1 box of pistachio instant pudding
6 cups cold milk
12 oz whipped topping

Make each flavor of pudding as directed on the package. Quickly fill each of the 4 small dessert dishes half full of pudding. Take the remaining pudding and add about 4 oz whipped topping and mix well. Pour this mixture over the original pudding. Refrigerate about an hour. Repeat this process with each flavor of pudding you choose. Serve on a footed platter.

Enjoy !

Super
Sports
Party

Kiki's BBQ Baked Beans

This wonderful recipe for baked beans can almost be a meal in itself. My niece Kiki has made it many times for our family and it has everything you need to satisfy your robust appetite.

Recipe

Here is what you will need:

1 lb sausage, browned
1 lb ground beef, browned
1 cup celery
2 large onions, diced
1 - 40oz can chili beans
2 - 3lb cans Bush's baked beans
1 can black beans
1 can lima beans
1 can waxed beans
1 can green beans
1 can kidney beans
1 tbsp mustard
1 cup dark brown sugar
1 can tomato soup or sauce
1 cup green pepper, chopped
salt and pepper

In a large dutch oven, roaster pan or crock pot, add all the ingredients (be sure to drain all the canned beans but not the chili beans or Bush's Baked Beans). Mix well. Bake at 350 degrees for 1-1/2 to 2 hours. In a crock pot, cook for 4 hours on low. Bake in the oven until they are thick and celery is tender. These are great made the day before and reheated.

Serve and Enjoy !

If you know anything about BBQ, it's all about the sauce. This recipe is not your typical smokey flavored BBQ. It is a little more sweet and sour, but I think you will like it.

BBQ Wings & Meatballs

Recipe

Ingredients:

1 cup dark brown sugar
1 cup white sugar
8 oz soy sauce
garlic powder

2 lbs fresh chicken wings

2 lbs frozen plain meat balls, thawed

tsp of crushed red pepper flakes, optional

In a small microwaveable mixing bowl, combine the sugars and soy sauce. Mix well. Dip the chicken wings in the sauce and place on a cookie sheet sprayed with cooking spray. Once all the wings are on the cookie sheet, drizzle a little more sauce over them and sprinkle lightly with garlic powder. Bake at 350 degrees for 1-1/2 hours, turning once or twice.

Do the same for the meatballs but use a 9x13 baking dish. Take any left over sauce and microwave for 5 minutes. Serve the wings and meatballs on a large platter with a side bowl of sauce.

Enjoy !

Corn & Black Bean Dip

Try this dip with a large bowl of Blue Tostada chips and an ice cold brew and you are in heaven. A zesty combination of corn, black beans and chilis is near perfection. All my friends love it.

Recipe

Here is what you will need:

2 cans of black beans, drained
1 - 10 oz can of corn relish
1/2 cup frozen corn, thawed
1 green pepper, chopped
1 can green chilis, chopped
1/4 cup Picante sauce
1/3 cup chopped cilantro
large bag of Blue Tostada chips

Combine all the ingredients (except the Tostada chips) together in a mixing bowl. Mix well. This is best when made the day before you need it. Serve with Blue Tostada chips.

Enjoy !

Mini pizzas are perfect for any type of party. I always make several varieties, to cover all the different taste buds out there.

This is the basic recipe. You can add all the different toppings to suit your taste.

You will need 2 twelve section muffin pans.

Mini Pizzas

Recipe

1 pkg regular dinner rolls that come in a refrigerated tube.
1 - 20 oz can of pizza sauce
2 cups mozzarella or monterrey jack cheese, shredded
Italian spices

Any combination of the following and about a 1/2 cup of each

green pepper
chopped onion
chopped olives
banana peppers
chopped mushrooms
artichoke hearts
pepperoni
chopped tomatoes
ground beef, cooked
bacon bits
hot peppers

Preheat oven to 350 degrees. Spray the inside of each muffin pan with cooking spray. Unroll the refrigerator rolls and break into 2-3 pieces to form thin round discs. Place in the bottom of each muffin space. Add a spoonful of pizza sauce and sprinkle with Italian spices. Add any combination of topping to your taste. Cover with mozzarella cheese. Bake in oven for 10-12 minutes until golden brown. Remove and serve immediately.

Enjoy !

Entertaining Tips   16

Dinnerware, Serveware and Bakeware   22

Serving Presentations   10

Theme Buffet Ideas   28

General Recipes

    Banana Splits   36
    BBQ Beef or Pork   81
    BBQ Wings and Meatballs   121
    Broiled Pork Tenderloin   99
    Bruschetta   49
    Champagne Party Punch   98
    Cheesy Potatoes   65
    Chicken & Veggie Kabobs   109
    Chocolate Mousse   56
    Chocolate Parfait   59
    Chocolate Raspberry   57
    Chocolate Tiramisu   58
    Classic Dressing   73
    Corned Beef & Cabbage   87
    Corn & Black Bean Dip   122
    Cranberry Salad   74
    Enchilada Casserole   40
    Famous Fatoush   51
    Fireworks Punch   80
    Five Cheese Mac 'n Cheese   89
    Fruit & Cream Trifle   103
    Fruit Infused Iced Tea   108
    Green Bean Casserole   76
    Homemade Caramel Corn   94
    Homemade del Salsa   42
    Homemade Guacamole   44
    Honey Orange Glazed Ham   62

Ice Cream Cake	32
Ice Cream Sundaes	34
Italian Caprese Salad	102
Kiki's BBQ Baked Beans	120
Kool Kabobs	48
Margaret's Deviled Eggs	64
Margarita Punch	41
Mashed Potato Casserole	70
Mini Pies	67
Mini Pizzas	123
Mini Quiches	116
Mixed Fruit Salad	82
Mixed Veggie Medley	66
Party Punch	35
Party Ring Surprise	33
Party Smoothies	37
Pesto Pizza	111
Pesto Spread	101
Potato or Macaroni Salad	83
Pudding Parfaits	117
Pumpkin Creams	95
Roasted Turkey	71
Salsa Chicken Casserole	106
Sassy Sangria	50
Scalloped Corn	75
Seafood Salad	52
Shamrock Cookies	88
Shamrock Punch	86
Sherbet Punch	114
Sloppy Joes	92
Spicy Meatballs	53
Sweet Potato Casserole	72
Taco Salad	45
Tea Sandwiches	115
Tomato Pudding	77
Tequila Taco Dip	43
Tropical Smoothies	107
Tuscan Flatbread	100
Turkey Casserole	110
Waldorf Salad	63
Witch's Bats & Brew	93

About the author.

ROBERT ZOLLWEG is a native of Toledo, Ohio and has been entertaining professionally for many years. Writing this cookbook on Buffet Style - Home Entertaining has been his dream and passion. He has worked in the tabletop industry for over 40 years. He designs glassware, flatware and ceramic product for the retail and foodservice industry. He has worked with all of the major retailers, including Bed Bath & Beyond, Pier One Imports, Macy's, Cost Plus World Market, Target, Walmart, Kohl's and Home Outfitters. He has worked most of his professional career for Libbey Glass in Toledo. Robert has traveled the world extensively looking for color and design trends and the right product to design and bring to the retail and foodservice marketplace. He is also an artist-painter in his spare time and works primarily with acrylic on canvass using bold colors. He has always had a passion for entertaining, so tasting parties and buffets will continue this passion. He currently lives in his historic home in Toledo's Historic Old West End and in the artistic community of Saugatuck, Michigan.

To find out more about Robert Zollweg, visit his web site at:

www.zollwegart.com

To find out about the product used in this book, visit the Libbey web site at www.retail.libbey.com

I hope you have enjoyed my buffet entertaining tips and recipes. I have written several cookbooks on entertaining and the books and products are all available at various retailers, as well as my web site.